Meyers
The dark birds

THE DARK BIRDS

Bert Meyers

THE DARK BIRDS

DOUBLEDAY & COMPANY, INC.
GARDEN CITY, NEW YORK
1968

Designed by Earl Tidwell

LIBRARY OF CONGRESS CATALOG CARD NUMBER 68–10577

PRINTED IN THE UNITED STATES OF AMERICA
FIRST EDITION

Thanks are due to the following periodicals in whose pages some of these poems have appeared: *Ante, Burning Deck, Choice, Kayak, The Literary Review.*

Earlier versions of some of these poems were first published in *Early Rain,* and are used by permission of the publisher, Alan Swallow.

I am grateful to the Ingram Merrill Foundation for a grant which enabled me to finish this book.

For Odette, Annette, and Daniel

Contents

I

The Dark Birds

15

They Who Waste Me

16

The Garlic

17

Eichmann

18

Pigeons

19

II

Madman Songs

23

III

Gulls Have Come Again

33

Funeral

34

A Tree Stump at Noon

35

The Accident

36

A Year in a Small Town

37

Winter

38

Windy Night

39

Sometimes

40

Icon

41

Lullaby

42

IV

One Morning

45

The Curse

47

The King at Evening

48

The Poet

49

Apprentice

53

When She Sleeps

54

From Any Hill

55

The Drive

56

V

Picture Framing

59

October Poem

60

In the Yard

61

Cigarette

62

Follow the Child

63

The Family

64

A Child's an Apple

65

Now I Sleep in the Afternoon

66

The Wanderer

67

Stars Climb Girders of Light

68

I

THE DARK BIRDS

The dark birds came,
I didn't know their name.

They walked in Hebrew on the sand
so I'd understand.

They sang, the sea flowed,
though no one made a road.

I shivered on the shore
when the water closed its door.

Then as I felt the birds return
to me like ashes to an urn,

and sunlight warmed the stones,
fire undressed my bones.

THEY WHO WASTE ME

When I ask for a hand,
they give me a shovel.
If I complain, they say,
Worms are needles at work
to clothe a corpse for spring.
I sigh. Whoever breathes
has inhaled a neighbor.

THE GARLIC

Rabbi of condiments,
whose breath is a verb,
wearing a thin beard
and a white robe;
you who are pale and small
and shaped like a fist,
a synagogue,
bless our bitterness,
transcend the kitchen
to sweeten death—
our wax in the flame
and our seed in the bread.

Now, my parents pray,
my grandfather sits,
my uncles fill
my mouth with ashes.

EICHMANN

This familiar form
displayed in the glass
is a sample of man
who can live
before he's born.

Because such creatures
read and write
without compassion,
your little time
and even your teeth
aren't safe.

You, when you see him,
should be frightened.
He comes from a large family
whose business prospers.

PIGEONS

Wherever I go to find
peace or an island
under palms in the afternoon
at midnight to pity my neighborhood
at dawn in the shrubs
to look for a child

I hear them
they fly by
applauding themselves
I see them
they pray as they walk
their eyes are halos
around a pit
they look amazed

Who are these that come
as a cloud to our windows
who rush up like smoke
before the town burns

You will find one
on a mountain
in a carpenter's shop
at home on the lawn
of an old estate
at the library
in the forehead of paradise

Whoever is mad
can accuse them
thousands were killed in a day

What happens to them
happens to me
when I can't sleep
they moan and I'm there
and it's still like that

II

MADMAN SONGS

I

People go home
to rest in vaults
curtains soothe their faults
bright windows show their money
I hated home
it caused me pain
cloudy days
and evenings came
I leaned against
the iron rain

2

Someone held me there was harm
now each word's an alarm
the man who looks so calm
will turn into a bomb
Woman daughter son
I wake up and put them on
they hide me from the law
My desire's a blade of grass
I trample as I pass
Fear me what I hate will fall

3

In summer small cones
of dirt beside a fence
erupt with the weddings
of the ants
a moth staggers from a shrub
People turn their sprinklers on
to watch the water girls
dance on their lawn
I don't go out
until they've all gone in
They might come near
with large damp wings
love and other things

4

When I don't sleep
the crickets weep

When I say
My life will pass
they scrape the dark glass

When the wall
begins to fall
where I strain
they file the chain

When I rise I wear
an orange shirt
A green woman
is rinsing her skirt
She imagines me

5

David's gone Goliath's strong
flocks of pebbles bleat
their little cries of light
fade where the leaves lie
dry harps near a stream

Jacob warmed a rock
the rock and Jacob dreamed
I'm burning I'm alone
everyone's a stone
I break my feelings on

6

I sat on the sidewalk
with my own box of chalk
and all day long I made
the whole world by myself
That's not the world they said

Then I rose at dawn
I put a label on
it wore me out by noon
All day I swung a brush
to see the buildings bloom

Just painting on a wall
won't change a man at all
or make the stone turn blue
So I sat down once more
What else could I do

7

People go home
Twilight's a glass
through which they pass
The carver calms
his arm and leaves
his passion in the grain
The one who ran
runs back again
We live in pain
The moon's an aspirin

III

GULLS HAVE COME AGAIN

Gulls have come again
to consider another beautiful death of the sun.

People were flowers that grew by the shore;
twilight takes them home,
they fade together at their tables.

In the tall green shops the pulleys of birds
lower the last light,
the eyelid of a shadow shuts the hills,
the sound of the ocean walks over the land.

Nobody wants to die.

FUNERAL

Surely a dead moth's
the skull of a tiny horse,
and the moon's a saint
who pities the sea.

Peace, peace to this child
of rain and light,
and the people who stay
holding candles and lilies,

tasting their tears,
naked in a dream,
over the long drawer
they've closed in the earth.

A TREE STUMP AT NOON

The light drips like oil
from an old machine;
a crow, big as a boot,
flies over the roofs
and begins to scream
at the men who build.
The huge root lies like a head
on a vacant field.

THE ACCIDENT

There's so much blood
the warm sun walks
like Christ upon it.

A needle's eye
in his tattered head
is losing his life's thread.

The crowd kneels down.

We see the tailor
in his chest
work overtime.

A siren blows.
The man tries
to straighten out
his body, like
a suit of clothes.

A YEAR IN A SMALL TOWN

1

Surrounded by flowers,
bees are drowning
in the housepainter's pot.

2

Today, I know
I haven't done as much
for this world as a tree.

3

Children bring home
stones instead of friends;
the blackbird has a golden eye.

4

Spring, that young man
is wearing the shirt
I was wounded in.

WINTER

The oils of autumn have dried,
branches crack the sky.
The walls of the world
are old, my friend . . .

Eat the wind's iron apple,
breathe razor blades;
drive home and bless
your photographs.

WINDY NIGHT

The sound of the wind
is the sound of a man
alone with himself
in the forest of sleep.

A tree, a mind holding on.

So many dry leaves fall,
then at last the rain.

SOMETIMES

You see a grey sky,
an infinite sidewalk:
no one's there and it's noon.
Silence opens an eye,
now you're a small cloud
heavier than a moon.

ICON

That burnished antique metal,
worn at the world's edge,
illuminates an orchard, a field,
and people planting there:
shadows the mind casts
to pose in a breathless valley.

As airplanes punch the town
with invisible fists of sound,
praise these walls before they fall
and those good buttons we push.
Tonight, we want the moon
to be dressed as a nurse.

LULLABY

Go to sleep my daughter
go to sleep my son
once this world was water
without anyone

IV

ONE MORNING

I told myself,
A single man's
like water where
nobody swims.
And I went out.

In gardens, doves
were broken jars
a wind blew through.
Beds of ivy
were spread with webs,

old underwear;
forgotten wives,
moths, or the wrong
figures of men,
lay at the roots.

While sparrows strained
their tiny springs
to live, I heard
how people damned
another day.

Later, I found
some blackberries
under a porch
and leaves as rough
as a cat's tongue.

THE CURSE

Because you lie there, curled
between the fingers of
her legs, expecting death,
though her green eyes close,
she smiles, and her face flows
to the edge of the world . . .

Be the cold water that comes
from the tap at dawn,
the sun, spilled on a lawn,
its egg broken in the dew.
Die, slowly, like the snow.
Fall apart in your own glue.

THE KING AT EVENING

What a sad face the lizard has.
I walk by in my clothes,
the lizard hides, ashamed.
What a sad face it has.
The day burns out in the grass.

Evening comes, made of silk,
the lizard grins and goes.
I rise, arranging my robes.
The odors of autumn build
sweet bedrooms in the air.

THE POET

I

They said, Go, rise each day
with her, become
the reliable dough a family needs.
I wouldn't. I walked away
from the kitchen, the store
she was building in her breast . . .
And everything grows dim
like the little stone
brought home from the shore.

2

What will I bring
if I come to your house?
A cold wind at the door,
bad dreams to your spouse.

There isn't a tree
in your backyard;
the lawns are plastic,
the chairs are too hard.

No, I wouldn't talk.
I'd be full of spite
and I'd strike my head
like a match that won't light.

3

Woman, mirror of all my sides,
I pass through you to the window.

When I lay my hand on the grass
forgive me if I call the earth my child.

4

Always poor, he knows
the crickets will leave him
small jars of money.

He waits, he admires a weed.
His dreams are addressed.

At night by his desk
he becomes a flower;
children are bees in his arms,
a little pain making honey.

APPRENTICE

Because
I love you
I've learned to be
this hammer that runs
all day like a horse
with its hoof in its head.

In the afternoon
my hands
lie down together
for a minute.

WHEN SHE SLEEPS

When she sleeps I rise.
The naked lightbulb burns
and makes the moths outside
beat against the screen.
A moth comes out of me.
It flies to the light,
then staggers back in pain
to rest in me again.
She sleeps and holds her peace,
though I'm consumed by this.

FROM ANY HILL

On any hill at night
lovers grow from the height.
A town's their Christmas tree.
She listens, her limbs are stirred
as he with only his word
opens packages of light.

They go wandering down
to the root of that town,
and day and night they hear
how each was a long shaft,
a hump on the other's back,
that brought them weeping there.

THE DRIVE

Because their bed was calm
and they'd never done
what they read about,
they drove to the hills,
left the car, and climbed
high over the shale
and spread her dress in the dirt.

Soft ceramic quail,
the natives there,
stared from the chaparral
while they groaned
and hurt themselves.
The heat made ants
bubble out of the ground.

The hill was a flower
that evening closed.
They were naked
and very small,
and they put on their clothes.
The car would give them back
their power.

PICTURE FRAMING

My fingers feed in the fields of wood.

I sand pine, walnut, oak,
and sweat to raise their grain.

Paints, powder, and brush
are the seasons of my trade.

At the end of the day
I drive home
the proud cattle of my hands.

OCTOBER POEM

October smokes a long cigar
and hangs its leather in the sun.
Metal on metal as the mind
feels the limber oil grow thin.

When I came home, after work,
I saw an old man mow his lawn.
Sweet rain fell from those blades, and death
smelled like a baby in its bed.

IN THE YARD

'he grasshopper goes for a ride,
s little sprocket spins
ver the earth.
[he lizard, five inches of stream,
lows under a board.
[he leaf runs from the cat.
A moth's a pharaoh in search
of a tomb full of light,
and a bumblebee explains
to the morning-glories
the joy of being a telephone.
Only the woman knows
what the man's for.

CIGARETTE

Often you light a fuse
to prove you won't explode.
All the smoke shows
the power that dies in you.

You sigh as you tap
your way to the end.
The hand is a blind child
called to the blackboard.

FOLLOW THE CHILD

Follow the child who feels
green gates of childhood close:
the enchanted eye will find
only what it knows,
and a grey-haired hunter stalk
that forest in his blood.

You too will see the firm
parental towers fall
at the quiet stroke;
the mighty adult crawl
to what it hates; and hear
a long, collapsing sky.

Then come those visitors
all wise men abhor—
but others let them in.
His own voice at the door,
the haunted man lies down.
He whitens in a white room.

THE FAMILY

The boy will grow and be a man.
He'll have no father then.

The girl, assuming womanhood,
will burn herself in bed.

The father leaves the house at dawn.
The mother turns her dream-world on.

Still, night brings them all together,
to shriek and shudder.

A CHILD'S AN APPLE

Those who are tall look down.
They show their keys,
the dead bird in their hands.
They open and close
volumes of doors.
They smile.
Their teeth are the stones
in the graveyard at noon.
They're always hungry
and when they love they bite.

NOW I SLEEP IN THE AFTERNOON

We gaze at the beautiful forms,
at the dark hair of delicate dials–
we want to hold and move the world.

Often as we extend our hands,
nothing happens: loose wires hang
from the plaster of our sleeves.

I have dreams in the afternoon
of khaki-colored leaves, and men
who fall, of cities like rain coming down.

THE WANDERER

The towns were tables, set
by the road each night.
A woman came to the door.
The builders needed help.
My sandwich was the sun
between two hills at noon.

What I've seen is true:
when the starved gull speaks
an old gate opens in the sky
and the fishing boats rise from the sea.

STARS CLIMB GIRDERS OF LIGHT

Stars climb girders of light.
They arrange themselves
in the usual place,
they quit before dawn,
and nothing's been done.

Then men come out.
Their helmets fill the sky;
their cities rise and fall
and the men descend,
proud carpenters of dew.

Man brief as the storm,
more than five feet of lightning,
twisted and beautiful.
Man made like his roads,
with somewhere to go.